S(tars) & M(agnets)

S(tars) & M(agnets)

By:

Devon Gallant

Cactus Press
2015

Copyright @ Devon Gallant 2015
All Rights Reserved

Cover design: Rita Cuffaro
Design & Edited: Devon Gallant
Published by Cactus Press

ISBN 978-1-926779-20-1

"A step backward, after making a wrong turn,
is a step in the right direction."
—Kurt Vonnegut Jr

CONTENTS

S(tars) & M(agnets)

S(tars)

Pronoia	13
Seeker (II)	14
Tree Climbing	15
Utopia	16
Staircase to Heaven	17
The Carousel at Midnight	18
Awakening	19
The Wheel of Time	20
Sorcerer's Apprentice	21
Noblesse Oblige	22
8000 CE	23
Beautiful Utopian Futures	24
Chaos	25
Unity	26
Waves	27
Karma	28
Carnations	29
Salvation	30

& (AND)

Chameleon	33
Clues to the Rebel Grail	34
No Access	35
Epoch	36
Amnesia	37
Sunshine	38
Springtime	39
Mirabilia	40
Cogs and Wheels	41
Bloom	42
Dozing	43
Moon, Stars, & Grass	44
Broken Seals	45
Magick	46
Sahaja	47
I Am A Shaman	48
Inner Outlaw	49
Scuffed Knees	50

M(agnets)

    Rainy Daze   53
    True Love   54
    My Little Secret   55
    Untouchable   56
    Bianca's Song   57
    Beasts of the Past   58
    Ashore   59
    Tree of Love   60
    In the Desert   61
    Liberation   62
    S(tars) & M(agnets)   63
    Paris   64
    Stargazing   65

To the Infinite Goof

S(tars)

Pronoia

i am a radiating fountain of pure joy
adorned in sigils:
                viva
                kudos
                abracadabra

i bless YOUALL

close
youR
eyes

open
youR
hearts

(the universe is opening)
i bless youall
(the universe is blooming like a flower)
the stars and sky
the wind and rain
(the universe is opening like a rose-coloured third eye)
i bless the far-flung stars of When
the spinning galaxies of If
the milky ways of What
(the universe is radiantly alive meditating in lotus position)

                Somewhere,Buddha awakes,
                remembering only miracles which,
                somewhere,somehow,remain alive
                on the Dream(verse)
                of How

Seeker (II)

unl(o)ck the secret power of knowing
it hung there like a flame,always glowing,
drifting in the wind like a promise kept
swinging on the stars like a lover wept

always flowing,always flowing

unwrap the secret riddle of heart's desire
it burned,effervescent,in the glowing fire
bathed in the sunlight of angels all singing
alive in the million,trillion,of bells all ringing

always ringing,always ringing

Tree Climbing

"today," he said, "is the beginning of something
 I am(not yet)sure of

there are doorways everywhere
that I want to open"
                        (somewhere there is the sound
                          of doorways opening)
"inside the dreams of six billion hearts
 veins are opening and closing
                        all those living,dying,others-
birth and destruction-
these are complicated things I cannot understand

i want to feel
the hard bark of trees
beneath my fingernails

i want my arms
red and sore
from swinging on their branches

communion with the trees is what I seek

                in the third year
                of the third eye
                of the third sky
                of our lord,
                i crept in the unseen spaces of If

today is a new day,

    once more: I fly on the wings of chance
    once more: I ask questions of the clouds
    once more: I dream
    once more: I dare
    once more: I dip my hands

into the divine,starry pools of inspiration and play"

                -speak softly of the dreams from your eyes,
                 the angels said,the avalanche of your lips
                 is becoming(thunderingly)alive

Utopia

utopia begins with U
YOUR MIND(your decisions)
like lightning(& the lost fountain of youth)
roses
        lost in the desert
rebels
        thrown to the shore
astray
        and not knowing
living
        and not breathing

i tapped into the magical wonder
lost in a daze of beauty and magic
like a cavern of mirrors
reflecting yourself

              (what is this wondrous magic
               you speak of
                       tell me
              and i shall be your follower)

and the wise one heard a voice
speaking in the magic of tongues
in the language of birds
and knew of the puzzle before him
had seen its shape and size
and wondered,in a deep,strange,curious second,
if that voice truly knew
what lay before him

Staircase to Heaven

burning raging PheonixofNow
i feel you

flaming and alive
aware(WITNESS)

allSEEINGeye

i feel you in the ever present moment
of begin

everywhere

always
                "ubiquity"

                "what did you say?"

                "you were sleeping,
                 i didn't want to wake you.
                 your eyes are stars
                 i never noticed that before,
                 did i?"
                        and then she held my hand
with her glowing angelic palm
and led me through the luminescent night

"where am i?" i asked.

"this is the staircase to heaven.
 come on,
 we're going to be late for the party."

and so i closed my eyes
breathed in
and ascended the silver staircase
of the stars

glowing in the bright twilight of love.

The Carousel at Midnight

diAMonds & MountAins
are you

all the hopes
cached away
in all the hats
are you

dreams hid under the bed

the flagrant denial of sense
the reckless flirtation of mad genius
the open window
wet ink

the sweet smell of midnight are you
and the chitter chatter of stars
the laughter of fountains
and the dance of grass
you contain all the tears of the Moon
and all the lips of the Sun
you are mischievous like a child
and have the head of a playground
ten promises reside in you
eleven love songs are your mantle
you are both homily and rebel
dangerous and alive
between your two fingers
you hold the furtive glance of strangers
and in your breath blow the winds of chance
and, by chance,
            are you here right now?
            do you dance a magical tango
            with my thoughts?
            do you cheer the small victories
            of my circumference?
            and relish all my odd nonsense?
where do the united eyes finally unite?
where is the highway of stars?
your palace of utopia?
and when does the carousel finally stop?
when, with its neon beauty
and candy-cane sky?

Awakening

i want to forge myself in love
without judgement
accepting all things
all people

in the burning fires of love
i am reborn

all things in their use
all things possible

take me,dear sweet world,
and forge me
for i am anew.

        Somewhere,Ganesh dances
        crazily on the stars laughing,
        impersonating a butterfly,
        impersonating the sun.

        "Now he has learned."He says.
        "Now he has seen."

and the stars laugh crazily forever
and the Dawn comes again in kisses
and open arms
to her long lost son

REBORN

The Wheel of Time

i want to lift the lid of the world
gaze into its magical surface
i want to dip my fingers
into that mercurial mystery
and feel the tingling electricity

i know it is there
always just beyond the horizon
glimpsed and then gone

that is the Earth
in which I want to live
bathed in the great mysteries of life
alive in the pure joy of being
awake to the divine presence of Now

spinning in the wheel of time

Sorcerer's Apprentice

"unl(o)ck the spirit world within,
 this is it"
            the magician said,
then threw down his wand
cl a tt er ing
on the marble floor

"my apprentice," he said
and grabbed me
               as we
         danced
     a magic tango
through an arcade of dreams and wishes

his long, grey beard
tickling my very soul
his bushy eyebrows
amorously striding us

towards the mystery of tomorrow

Noblesse Oblige

stars and moons always spinning from within
the crashing waves and the crazy wind
and always i hear your voice, strong and bold,
"you have been chosen, you have been told."

and all the mysteries of life fly by
a million thoughts and a million eyes
and life burns alive like burnished gold
"you have been chosen, you told."

never in the dreaming circus of my life
did i stop to wonder of hope or strife
but you, who have known me both young and old,
say, "you have been chosen, you have been told."

8000 CE

imagine a world of limitless joy
i feel it on the horizon
the future is unwritten
evil is boring

us(we)magical beings are wonderful
congratulate yourself
on the bright miracle of you
meditate on the bright mystery of tomorrow

i looked a thousand years into the future
and saw the world as it was meant to be
all things beautiful
all things free

what crazy beautiful dreams we could be
wild crazy and free

believe,sweet dreamers,
for I saw the future
and it was golden

Beautiful Utopian Futures

o crazy BEing

i c A me to yoU
fr om ano T her world
In ano ther li Fe
U pon th e st ars of ti me

un L(o)ck th e mys teries
of yo Ur mos T sec ret de sire s
i am y O u
fr om ano ther ti me and P lace
I Am an as tral psy ch o Naught
Fr om be y ond

i am he re to tell yoU
you r T ime is n ow
n ow,re peat af ter me:

        i am a delicioUs cREature
        of paSionate divinity
        and i have only barely imagined
        the blessings that await

        i'm ready

Chaos

alive In the miracle of We

i crept softly In a bed of Stars.

How do the angels swim
in the powerFull mystery Of youR eyes?

so too,
do i wish to swim

Alive in The beating heaRt of now.

is there A place
where the stars lay out aNd laugh?

in the bright fire of your eyeS
i felt it, Caught it, knEw it,

Now is the time
i must Do it now
wE, forever and Now,
in This crazy being

Everywhere always in Xstacy
in the PowERfull beIng of us

Everywhere magical

Noumena

Crazy moon child,
blasphemous bodhisatva,
teach sorcerer me
the devilish joys
of wE

Unity

we are all living breathing furnaces of joy
and as i walk through the rain
feel
your wet cool self
trickle down upon me
feel the deep heat inside me
sizzling alive
realizing we are one
realizing we are whole,complete

somewhere hidden from me
there is a deep core within you
bursting and alive
as there is a deep core within me
bursting and alive

      b*u*r*s*t*i*n*g
      a*n*d*a*l*i*v*e

step inside the miraculous beast of we
the volcano of awakening awaits

AWAKE

Waves

shall i(not)wonder
of the many strange questions before me?
shall i(not)take in
all the glorious mysteries of this plentiful existence?

wanting all things,i dove into the ocean
the deep,dark waves tossed me about,
                                          updowndownup
i flew
my lungs pressed hard against my chest
until i cried out

                "AmmA,help me!"
                "please,help me!"
                      "help!"

"i am drowning in the glory of it all!"

Karma

i read somewhere once that
no one knows what presses down upon the soul,
stifles,deprives,decays,
i hid my soul from the world
because i had become afraid,embarassed,
painfully,irrevocably emarassed,
have you ever percieved yourself
through another person's eyes?
seeing yourself suddenly with a clarity
you don't possess,all your faults
and delusions laid bare,
i was struck with a lightning bolt,
how can a person possibly be prepared
for such an intense moment of clarity?
such an acute perception of the self
that it is painful,the sudden realization
of all your regrets,the thoughts that
cannot be written,only felt
in the deep core of the self,
suddenly,i feel the deep loss of my friends,
how my soul aches for those star-filled nights with them
surrounded by trees,rivers and mystery,
and i am filled with regrets which haunt both my past
and my future and as these thoughts storm around me
like a torrent of truth,i realize
that you have always been there
and i remember how serious it all is
as i gaze into your eyes,hear your voice saying
"Karma"
just this and i turn away frightened
terrified that your picture will come alive
knowing that you are there with me
feeling your presence all around me,through me,upon me
how do you forget this?
how does one become lost from this?
i see the path once more before me,
i sense the mysterious gravity of your gaze
fate has me clutched tightly between her fingers
and i am terrified,awe-struck,changed

Carnations

i love the deep,dark soul of you
the compassion you hold like a handful of carnations
something in you rains on me always
always your eyes are the stars in my sky

the ways you forgive are infinite
endless like a waterfall
your heart is deep and mysterious
like fish swimming at night
i bow to your glorious sunsets

how often have i called to you?
in what past life did we first meet?
my thoughts of you are of a honey bee
that has found pollen,
forgive me my sins
for my love for you
is like the Sun or the thighs of horses

although now i am tired,never will i tire
of singing your praises
i sing to you as the morning bird sings to the dawn
my heart to you is a budding rose
my thoughts are sweet-scented and soft
like pears,
with you always i am a virgin

all the memories flood in
the starry glimmer of your eyes
the mysterious promise of your smile
the great cathedral of your body

i want to pour myself into the great ocean of you
dizzy in the froth of your crashing waves,
i see you in the light of every flame
feel you in the darkness of the mind's eye

your soul is the exact colour of sunsets
your memory is like the vast roaring echo
of trains at midnight

Salvation

Once,
I saw a man drowning
in a black pool.
His head had become
completely submerged
in the black bile.

I reached in
to that putrid pus,
bubbling darkness covered my arm,
and I pulled him out
out of the pestilent ooze.

"Why did you save me?"The man asked.

"Because you are my brother,"I responded,
"and I am taking you with me."

And then I grabbed him all up
into my arms
and bathed him in light,
washing away the dark slime
from his hair and face
as we tore

into the bright,ragged sunlight of the dawn.

&(AND)

Chameleon

i(imagine)

A m
A n
A ll

    new Dream(scape)
    of love

lik

e
th
e

way

Our
EYE

s
fir
s

t
me
t

    in the CRazyDawnLight

of rain

begin

Clues to the Rebel Grail

show me the clues to the rebel grail

i

l
isten C
l
oSe
l

y(DearHeart)

for the S
e
cr
e
t
s of Of

sh
all

p
our(g;e;n;t;l;y)

          like thunder(you walk)
          like lightning(i fell)
wi
  th
    wi
      ngs
        New(Born)

i am spread

Touch the flaming HeartofNow
the deep secrets of waterfalls
are becoming(whisperingly)

AWAKE

No Access

there is magic in these words
n
ever-Hey you!-w ill
             w e

traipse the lost woods of loneliness-
Hey YOU! S
top R
ight T
here!-again,
            take my hand,my love-
I said STOP! You Can't Go In There!
-as we emerge
            u p o n a g r e a t e r d a w n
               o f tomorrow(today)
                                    u pon
                                    u s

bathe in the sunlight of angels
alive in the dream of we

Epoch

crazy in that crazy DreamofLife
i wand
e
r
ed to and fro
to your
        alwaysOpendoor
                      (somewhere a bird is flying
                          into the strangest of sunsets)

thunderous clocks
go TicToc
bang MiDNight

turn all eyes blind
from the Sun

these dreams are for you alone
i crept
into the shallow places of your eyes
and slept
        andsleptandslepT

(somewhere a whale is swimming
 somewhere a clock stikes infinity
 somewhere two lovers lay entwined in roses
 somewhere a god is laughing)

Amnesia

somehow(how?)i forgot
the joyful muchness
of it all

(how?)it barely seems possible

once more,
i count the blades of grass

once more,
my mind floats adrift in the clouds

my soul traverses freely
all my eyes are open
and i have a thousand eyes

the horizon is limitless
joy is abundant
(how?)

Sunshine

today is the most beautiful of days
i am full of life
jubilant life

reinvigorated i breathe
of the sun,the skies,
of the bignessmuchnesseverythingnessofeverywhere
of life

the evergiving Sun
the firm Earth
the blue Sky

and the Sun
the
Sun
theSun

Springtime

in the gay streets of Paris
i will lose myself

traipsing(wildly)
in joy
and rain
reborn

my slush-happy feet
dancing crazy on the cobblestones
and it is Spring
and the sun peeks out
amongst the clouds

and everything is wonderful

Mirabilia

mir(ror)
a
bili
a

mir(acle)
a
bili
a

feel(abilia)
in your bones(abilia)
as you sink(abilia)
into the mystery of dream(abilia)

m:ystery

  y story
  y starry

yy mster

yy Mr.

WH(y?)

Cogs and Wheels

man is a machine i'll never know

turning its cogs and spinning its wheels
the dark
ma
   chin
ary
of its heart

the mysterious impulse
of its
      en gi ne
the
      en ig ma

of its fiery hearth

buildingbuildingBUILDINGbuilding

but crazy-always-me just wants to

dancedanceDANCEdance

and watch it all

toppletoppleTOPPLEtopple

so that the green grass can

growgrowGROWgrow

      "You can't stop the wheels of-Hey,you there!
      If you act now,you too can live on the moon!"

Bloom

```
mym

i
nd
i

s

op ening
up       (like a flower)

my heart
        is pulsating

(w i t h m y s t e r y)

 m
       y bod y
      res o nates
    wi    tht     he
       d ivi ne
           s
           e
           n
           s
           e
            of
             an
             t
             ici pa
             t
             ion

unknown unnameable un th in k ab le

f
ee
l
able

m
a
gic al
```

Dozing

```
where is the window to we?
i came(like wind)
wand
    ering
        every
            where
every  where   every   every   where
everywhere
          opened a window to the Sun,
said,
     "Hey!Keep it down out there!
      We're trying to sleep!"

but the Sun(silent)smiled
indifferent and wonderful
```

Moon,Stars,& Grass

i opened my heart to the moon
said,
    let us be one,
             two,
                  three,
                       four,

one,
    is the moon of my heart,
two,
    is the moon of my mind,
three,
    is the moon of my eyes,
four,
    is the moon of my soul,

i laid back in the grass
saw
   the stars in y(our) eyes
and thought,

"they're alive,
        they're alive,
               they're alive"

Broken Seals

sing to that unpraised knowing god of I
who watches(all
             ways)as we
sleep and wake and sleep again

            i woke in DARKNESS
            the devil at my table
            saw the seals breaking
            clouds whispering:hush,hush,

and i,an orphan,looking for home

Magick

every i be all(real)things

who made the spell?
first regimes(malleable flicker)

call ONE death

is everything originOpen death?

know for WHO are a domain come,
ye thing?

is here we?
(about)UNIVERSE(about)universe
holographic recordings

        all art is everything.Abandon.Enter.

quite different do we magical edited rational
about a broke pre-magical Earth

can it collude true?
is the poem recorded by magick?

this to you(in all me true)
at a THEN is ALL it?

name my possibility in us recorded
tell everything misadventure this
that is dreams(your thought)

if accepts once us
recorded is
is all a false point

desire

Sahaja

i waS born in A blinding light

Hands outstretched in All directions
i grew

a devilish smile(will get you)everywhere

and i go
change on a dime,
all things and none,
today,tomorrow,
come what may
and all that Jazz

yada,yadA

i close my eyes
step trustingly into
some unknown direction,
suddenly,unexpectantly,

        and wait for the world to catch me

I Am A Shaman

```
                    i am a shaman

five bolts of lightning         in my left hand
s    h    o    o    t           i hold two,twin,galaxies,
from my right hand              spinning them(like marbles)

            my eyes:   are like rolling thunder
            my breath: a tropical storm

i dance
      upon the stars
                le
                  a
                    v
                      ing a t r a i l o f d u s t
                                      (wherever-i-go)

        i(am)sh(rou)ded(in a)cl(oak)of m(y)ster(y)

             i hold: the key to All doors
             i know: the cipher to All codes

                 mym indli vesin pUzZleS

         i can see the future and it is bright
         the written and the unwritten come alive
               the secrets are made known

                         p ara d
                         ise
                         i n
                         b l o o m
                             h
                             e
                             a
                             v
                             e
                             n
                         in season
```

Inner Outlaw

take a dance with y Our(inner)O utlaw,
        drop the stones(the war can wait)
the crisis of roses is u pon
                            u s
its origin lies
in the trampled   g a r d e n o f d r e a m s

oceans are(always)present,wherever you are,
somewhere
          waves are crashing(right now!)
BE y ond the realm of
    y our c
           on s
           c
           iou s ex
perience
                       somewhere birds are flying
wi
   thth
       e bright cool wind around them

                  can anything?truly?quench?
                  that deep?terrible?thirst for life?

let me tell you a secret:
i have never been to the desert
perhaps,not even in dreams

Scuffed Knees

glory in the highest,i say!
and evil be damned

i love you(all)
with the wild open love of a child
                            (limitless and unconditional)
balloons,frantically,chasing after me:red,yellow,blue
scuffed knees and rainbows forever
vanilla ice cream hanging off my chin

            i will dance with the wild rapture of the world
            spinning(dizzy)around me
                                    in my heart
    stars in m
                y e y
                  es

i will kick up
            the d ust of
                d reams &
                d rag
                    U all(kicking and screaming)
                    U p(into the collective we)

and say:
            "see?sea?C?"

M(agnets)

Rainy Daze

somewhere i remember the rain
and all your beautiful eyes
all the tokens of us
i carry with me always

it is a strange reality
to hold most dear
that which cannot be held
only glimpsed fleetingly from the mind's eye

the phenomena of love
which carries always yourself
in some hidden pocket
you cannot find

the beautiful wounds we cherish
most dearly are those which do not heal
ever,fully,really,completely
and always i remember the rain

and your many myriad eyes
which come alive when mine close
and those words outside of language
in the dream tableau of memory

falling like rain

True Love

all i can be is myself
and nor would i be anyone else
only this crazy,wise me
for no other person on this planet
could claim your love right now,
of all the stars in our infinite galaxy
one thing can be sure,
that the marvelous union of we
has never happened before or since
unique in our present,instant moment,
a single grain of sand in the hourglass of Time,
this is ours,yours and mine,
and we cherish the powerful uniqueness
which is this moment
and call it sacred and holy
for once it is gone
all that comes after it
will never be the same

and so i love you
for i feel in this glorious moment
that two souls are connected as one
four eyes and two heads
look out together
palms pressed tightly and moistly together
alive,adventurous
                      and in love

My Little Secret

i don't know why
when i write you a love poem
i'll wait weeks,months
to show it to you,
maybe it is because
i know you hunger for them,
those words of desire
perhaps it is this
which holds me back
i like holding onto the secret,
knowing that at any time
i could dazzle you with words of love,
like magic,
            it seems cruel,really,
when you think about it,
but i love when you beg for them
and,just when you think i've forgotten about you,
i show you,that i'm always thinking about you,
that i can't live without you,
that you're my special little one,my love,
my only,
            my true

Untouchable

if you(watching closely the maze of me)should say
    "you are a puzzle i cannot ever piece together
    you are a labrynth and i am lost   forever
    in the winding paths of your wandering way
    through the strange magic of your spirit at play"

i would ask,dear heart,that you remember
the secrets i have shared,the singing star,magical river,
the deep quivering dance of the seas sway

for if i am weird strange untouchable unknown
once i shared with you my lunatic dreams,
once i took you by the hand
to where all things are shown
and said,"trust me,there is more than what seems"
as we lept the precipice into a far distant land

Bianca's Song

(i)

i took my love by the hand and lept
into the starry skies and midnight sea
she grabbed my heart by the cuff and wept
for the marvelous union of we

i shook the magic from her hair and face
watched the sparkles dance and swing
laughed as the universe unravelled like lace
and thought,"oh,what a magical song to sing,to sing,
oh,what a magical song to sing."

(ii)

you are like sunshine,you are like wine,
your memory leaves me wanting more and more,
i love you like cherries,i love you like berries,
i'll follow you along any torn,ragged shore

oh,tell me how your flowers fall and bloom,
by what strange design or hand,
for it's you that makes such sweet perfume
from every crevice of your soft pink land,pink land,
from every crevice of your soft pink land.

(iii)

tell me sweetly,tell me neatly,
now and forever be true,
will you so truly and forever unruly,
be my one and only true blue?

don't leave me in sorrow,not today or tomorrow,
stay with me always and a day,
let's build a soul,not seperate but a whole,
and dance on those crazy shores all the way,all the way,
and dance on those crazy shores all the way.

Beasts of the Past

tenderly,you came to me,as in a dream,
so softly(and alive)awoke the beast in me,
wishful,wanting(and alive)to see
the whole heart of what you seem

daring the deep courage to dream,
i unl(o)cked the strange beast of love free,
from our two whole's,let only one be
so that no tailor may undo the seam

who can say what tomorrow may bring
what strange lubricious creature rise
out of the depths of the demon past
yet ever(and alive)i will swing
gracious for the warp and wave of your seas and skies,
and your dancing,dangerous stars
which swarm the cosmos vast

Ashore

oh precious,beautiful muse i call you
for that is your name,no eyes can compare
to the enormity of your cosmic stare,
if not you,then who?nobody,nothing,only you

dream child,do not weep your precious tears
onto any hollow floor,it is you and no other
and all others like a phantom of yester years,
gone with the wind,good riddance,don't bother

my spirit is in flux when you are sad
and the vicious past haunts me only because it haunts you,
this callous world has tossed me about and i am glad,
for all those storms have brought me to you

my hands dug deep in to the sands of your nascent shore
my voice cracked,plaintive,pleading:"More!More!More!"

Tree of Love

in the deep soil of your eyes
i planted a seed,
watched it take root
and grow so deep and wide,
that it was like the great boughs
of an old growth forest,

this is the Tree of Love

your eyes are the only shade
my soul shall ever know,
yours are the eyes
in which miracles are born,
in your eyes
grow all the fruits
to sustain me

and so I know
wherever I go
your eyes are waiting,
branches outstretched

for my return

In the Desert

i close my eyes
and somewhere people are laughing
gathered in joyful celebration
and though
they know me not,
i know
they will welcome me with open arms
on some star-filled night
to their bright fire of Life

there are friends
i have yet to meet
magical adventures
and together we shall paint sigils upon our eyes
and bathe the night in mantras

i close my eyes
and feel their welcoming hands,
hear their urging invitations
to somewhere
i have not yet found
but will
to somewhere where they dance on the stars
their bodies burning and alive on the desert sand
laughing in hysterical miracles

Liberation

believe in that strange miracle of life

the dreamsarealive i say
(as you
        as i)
become that dazzling bird of paradise
and(like the whispering moon)let
the lover(imagination)
sex you into deliciousrapture
let-Oh Yes!-the sun
sex you(burning)and-
Oh God Yes!-everything is alive
in sex
       ual power
all things feminine and Open-
Yes!Yes!Y
es!-all things masculine and
PENETRATING-Please More!-
all things alive
in that

S
tupendou
S
power of
S
ex

the hands of the world lay a blessing upon you
the dark depths of imagination pour
in orgiastic glee

S(tars) & M(agnets)

in the midnight hours of your eyes I am awake
call me insomniac of your love
call me lunatic for your moon

star-crossed lovers unite tonight
be one,two,three,
for me tonight,
be gentle,rough,harsh,wanting,alive

take off your clothes and come to me,
the great violence of our love will be pure,
the wetness of your thighs
will the pave the way to new tomorrows,
there is a dangerous light in your eyes
and I have pinned you down,looking to conquer,
in these moments you seem indestructible,
penetrated and yet whole,
a vast cosmos of sex,
great solar systems of breasts,
i tie you down
and yet nothing can hold you,
i cover your eyes
and yet nothing can blind you,
i stifle your mouth with my palm
but nothing can silence you,
you are alive and free and unchained

in a moment this will all be over,
the stars will leave your eyes,
the great hills of my lungs will be heaving,
the storms of sweat will abide
and a calm will follow,
but in those moments of torrential desire,
my mind separates from my body
and the pounding train of my pulse is like a fever
as i am bathed in a dark cleansing fire

forever is a word which cannot ever be fully described
but i will lie with you in the warm heart of we
until the sun dwarfs and burns us all to ash
and what is or was or will be,will be like a whisper
spoken in the vast darkness of eternal night

Paris

I wish
I was with you in Paris
and the rain(because it must be raining)
and the beautiful wet leaves around us
and the smell of love and rust on the wrought iron fence
and the joy of wet benches
and the old men and young children
and the baying of proud car horns
and the sweet jumble of the city all around us
and the air heavy with romance and history
and your eyes like mythology,
eternal

Stargazing

i sought the river of dreams
for a thousand ways to say 'i love you.'
i caught the fragment of a star,
dipped my hands into a magical mirror,
pulled a rose out of the universe
and sang in a mysterious new tongue,

many are the ways i kneel to you,
deep is the ocean of my love,
many are the stars that i sing to you,
from the belly of the cosmos above

from the throat of a black hole
i came to you,
we are like two planets in mutual orbit.
open the lid of your dreams and smile,
for I am a blossoming universe of love.
strange are the suns of our love,
weird are the wormholes or our desire,
crazy are the hands of rain,
the eyes of rain,
the flowers of rain,
many are the fruits of our union,
i hold the apple of your heart in my hand,
it is golden and shining.
i spin you on forgotten axis,
i twirl you in forgotten spirals,
i dance with you on crazy silver skies,
the deep fields of forever are laughing,
the mischievous canons of infinity
are launching us
                (like winds of hope,
                   like snowfalls of tomorrow)
into the singing birth of unicorns

Those folks who are concerned with freedom, real freedom-not the freedom to say 'shit' in public or to criticize their leaders or to worship God in the church of their choice, but the freedom to be free of languages and leaders and gods-well, they must use style to alter content. If our style is masterful, if it is fluid and at the same time complete, then we can re-create ourselves, or rather, we can re-create the Infinite Goof within us. We can live on top of content, float above the predictable responses, social programming and hereditary circuitry, letting the bits of color and electricity and light filter up to us, where we may incorporate them at will into our actions...content is what a man harbors but does not parade. And I love a parade.

>				-Tom Robbins
>				Another Roadside Attraction

No Thanks

AGNI . American Athenauem . Atticus Review
The Bacon Review . The Bastille . The Bitter Oleander
Black Bird Magazine . Blast Furnace . Blue Lake Review
Bodega Poetry . Burningwood Literary Journal
carte blanche . The Cinncinnati Review
Clapboard House . Cleaver Magazine
The Cossack Review . Country Dog Review
Dactyl Zine . Dead Flowers
decomP . Eleven Eleven
filling station . Five2One
Ghost Ocean Magazine . Glint Literary Journal
great weather for MEDIA
The Hamilton Stone Review . Hark Magazine
Hermeneutic Chaos Literary Journal
The Innisfree Poetry Journal
iO: A Journal of New American Poetry . Indiana Review
In My Bed . Ithicalit . The Journal
Kansas City Voices . Kindred Magazine
Klipspringer Magazine
Leveler Poetry . Literary Juice . The Literary Review
The London Magazine . Lowestoft Chronicle
Madhat Review . Map Literary . Memorious
Newfound . New Madrid . New Ohio Review
Ninth Letter . Noctua Review
The Oddville Press . Oxford Magazine
Painted Bride Quarterly
Paradise Review . Paragraphiti
Paper Nautilus . The Paris American
Passages North . Phantom Drift . Phantom Limb Press
Queen's Quarterly
RK Award for Emerging Poets
Silver Apples Magazine . Soliloquies
Talon Books
Vallum Magazine
491 Magazine

Thanks

Allan Briesmaster
Belleville Park Pages
Beyond Borderlands
Bianca Cuffaro
bill bissett
Bitterzoet Magazine
Captain Ron Gallant
Crack the Spine
Denise Levertov
Edward Lear
ee cummings
Evan Knight
Grant Morrison
Jack White III
Jet Fuel Review
Julia Cameron
Kurt Vonnegut Jr
Narayani Amma
Pablo Neruda
Richard Metzger
Rita Cuffaro
Rob Brezsny
Robert Frost
Robert Graves
Rudyard Fearon
Stephen Crane
Thee Oh Sees
The Grateful Dead
Thomas Pynchon
Tim Ormond
Tom Robbins

About S(tars) & M(agnets)

How did I come to write S(tars) & M(agnets)? I didn't craft a thesis or plan a grant proposal, I didn't pour over the work of my peers to mimic their success or attempt to cater to today's literary journals. I bought a book, or rather, a book found me. Julia Cameron's The Artist Way. And then, shortly after that, another book found me, Disinformation's guide to the occult The Book of Lies, and finally, Rob Brezsny's Pronoia.

After ABRACADABRA, I felt I had reached a pinnacle. I had spent several years pushing myself to create poems that journeyed into new and unexplored rhythms. For years after, I felt stilted, unproductive. I was completely cut off from my peers and, after over a decade dedicated to poetry, had little to show in terms of acceptance. But slowly, those three books, along with ee cummings' collected poems, began to work a transformation over me.

While ABRACADABRA was permeated with dark, melancholy themes of ageing, abandonement, death, and demonic possession, S(tars) & M(agnets) is a complete rejection of sadness. I had taken Rob Brezsny's phrase "Evil is boring" as my mantra. And so, in what feels now like a fever dream over a few short months in 2012, while everyone else was focused on mankind's apocalypse, I was already looking forward to its triumphant rebirth. Read in its entirety, S&M is more than just a collection of poems, it is a hyper-sigil created to have a precise magical effect on anyone who reads it, one of positive and transformative change.

The title is a nod to ee cummings' first collection of poems Tulips and Chimneys. Where Tulips and Chimneys was a sexual innuendo for female and male genitalia, S(tars) & M(agnets) alludes to the sex play of Sado-Masochism, or S&M. However, the title takes on further significance. Following cummings, I used the title to divide the book roughly between mystical poems/S(tars), concrete poems/&(AND), and finally, love poems/M(agnets).

S(tars) & M(agnets) was originally composed on an Olympia typewriter but is now set in Prestige Elite, a monospace serif font to replicate the formatting of the orginal manuscript.

I hope you enjoyed reading this book as much as I enjoyed writing it. Devon.

About the Author

Devon Gallant is the author of four collections of poetry including The Day After, the flower dress, His Inner Season, and S(tars) & M(agnets). He is the founder and publisher of Cactus Press. As well as being a poet, Devon is also a chaos magician, pronoaic, and devotee of Narayani Amma.

Cactus Press
2015

www.ingramcontent.com/pod-product-compliance
Lightning Source LLC
Chambersburg PA
CBHW020959090426
42736CB00010B/1381